Sa

Castle

Richard Bell

WILLOW
ISLAND
EDITIONS

Also by Richard Bell
Around Old Horbury
Around Old Ossett
Waterton's Park
Thornes Park
Coxley Valley
Malham Magic

Village Walks in West Yorkshire
(Countryside Books)
Yorkshire Rock
(British Geological Survey)

© Richard Bell 2001
Published by Willow Island Editions,
41 Water Lane, Middlestown,
Wakefield, WF4 4PX
www.willowisland.co.uk

First published 2001
Second edition 2002

ISBN 1-902467-05-1

CONTENTS

Sandal Castle

Gate-
house

Well Tower

Keep

Drum
Towers

Barbic

Motte

Curtain
Wall

Bake
hou

Outer Moat

Outer Defences

Perspective view not to scale; earthworks
approximately 260 x 150 yards (240 x 140m)

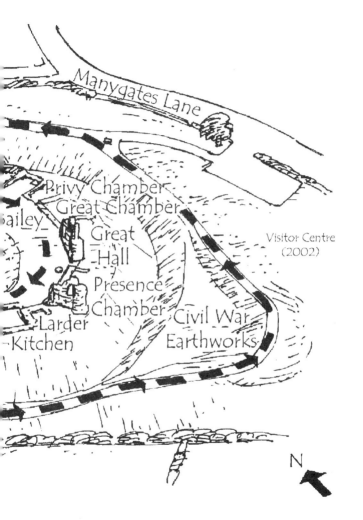

Manygates Lane

Privy Chamber
Great Chamber
Bailey
Great
Hall
Presence
Chamber
Larder
Kitchen

Civil War
Earthworks

Visitor Centre
(2002)

N

Gatehouse

THE GATEHOUSE was built in about 1250 to replace a timber bridge and gate. If attackers got across the drawbridge, through the outer gate and succeeded in breaking through the portcullis they would find themselves in an angled sloping passage (added *c.*1290) which twisted to the left. This made it difficult to get a straight run at the inner gate with a battering ram, especially as the defenders of the castle had the opportunity to rain down arrows and rocks from above.

A janitor or porter lived in the gatehouse, or in a small lodge attached to it which stood just inside the castle on the right.

The front of the gatehouse was extended sideways with stone 'book-ends' in the 15th century. You can see the change in the stonework.

Battle of Wakefield

c. 1460

RICHARD PLANTAGENET *(1411-1460)* Duke of York and Lord of the Manor of Wakefield led several thousand of his men out through this gatehouse on the afternoon of 30th December 1460. Lancastrian forces had ambushed a foraging party which included one of his sons, Edmund, Duke of Rutland. A second, larger, force of Lancastrians surprised Richard, cutting him off from the castle. He was killed during, or shortly after, the battle which took place on fields in the Manygates and Portobello area, between the castle and the river. A Victorian memorial *(1897)* next to the Manygates Adult Education Centre now marks the spot where he fell.

The Well Tower

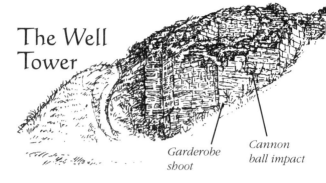

Garderobe shoot

Cannon ball impact

RICHARD III, *(1452-1485)* son of Richard, Duke of York, had the Well Tower of the keep rebuilt in the 1480s as a three storey 'block-house', capable of being held independently, even if other parts of the castle fell into enemy hands. It had its own water supply; fourteen stone steps in the basement led down to the well, which was at least 120 feet (37 m) deep. This basement room had its own fireplace. Traces of a garderobe shoot indicate that there was a privy in a room above. Smooth-faced stone cladding, known as ashlar, was used to convert the original semi-circular tower into the new polygonal design.

A chapel, dedicated to St Nicholas, with a belfry was probably at the top of one of the other towers of the keep.

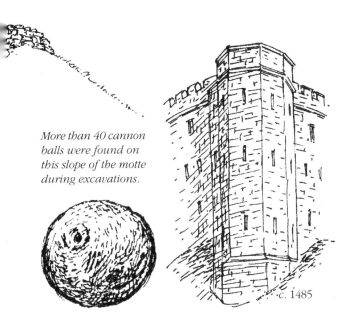

More than 40 cannon balls were found on this slope of the motte during excavations.

c. 1485

By 1566 the keep was already partly ruined, but even in 1645 there was enough of the Well Tower left standing for Royalist forces to defend it as a strongpoint during the civil war siege *(see page 31)* of the castle. The gash in the north west wall of the tower was the result of a cannon ball impact. As Parliamentary forces continued their bombardment, reducing parts of the keep to rubble, the Royalists were obliged to dig a trench across the top of the motte to reach the Well Tower in safety.

Motte

IT HAS BEEN estimated that it took a team of 100 men two years to complete the earthworks at Sandal. The motte and bailey were constructed, probably soon after 1106, on a natural ridge of sandstone, the Oaks Rock. Soil and rocky debris from the moat were piled up in layers to form the motte. This stood 33 feet (10m) above the original ground level with the moat a further 23 feet (7m) deep around it. The motte was 130 feet (37m) in diameter, 48 feet (15m) at the summit.

Hastings, 1066

Keep

c. 1250

IN THE 13th century a circular double-walled stone keep was built on the motte to replace a timber watchtower. It had four semi-circular towers, two of them built together as single unit to form a gatehouse. Its four storeys included prison cells on the lower floors and living accommodation above. You've got to imagine something the height of Wakefield's Ridings Centre perched on the motte. The keep's circular inner courtyard may have been partially, or completely, roofed over.

The 13th century **curtain wall**, which replaced a timber stockade, stood 20 feet (6m) high. It looped around the bailey crossing the moat to connect with the keep at both ends. A wall walk ran along its length, but appears to have stopped short of the keep.

11

Bailey

THE CRESCENT-SHAPED bailey, 230 feet (71m) long by 170 feet (52m) wide, was constructed as an outer line of defence for the motte. Traces of ridge and furrow plough strips, similar to those which can still be seen in nearby Manygates Park, were uncovered in the 1970s by archaeologists as they dug a trench down through the bailey. Pollen grains from cornfield weeds and crops are further evidence that the Norman bailey was raised over a part of the open fields of the village of Sandal. A shallow ditch and hollow with a scatter of flint tools found beneath the bailey suggest that Mesolithic hunters camped here about 7,000 years ago.

The 12th century bailey was edged by an earthen bank, which was probably topped by a timber palisade. Most traces of this bank were destroyed when the stone curtain wall *(left)* was built in the 13th century.

As you entered the bailey through the gatehouse in Tudor times you'd pass, on your right, the Porter's or Steward's Lodgings (a half-timbered house) then, on your left, the more imposing Constable's Lodging *(above, in 1562)*, topped with decorated chimney pots and finials. The bailey well is seven feet (2m) wide and was originally at least 40 feet (12m) deep.

Two substantial privy (lavatory) shafts *(above, right)*, one of them 26 feet (8m) deep, were constructed in the 1480s, between the Constable's Lodgings and the curtain wall. They are now capped by modern iron grills but were originally each topped by a wooden or stone seat.

Barbican

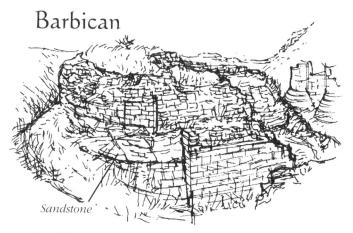

Sandstone

IN 1270-71 work was in progress on the barbican. Graves' (local officials') accounts record that masons and carpenters had been hired and payments made for supplies of stone, gravel, lime (for mortar), iron and timber (used for scaffolding as well as for construction). A mention of 'targes' suggests that its battlements were equipped with timber flaps to give protection to archers.

The D-shaped tower contained a guardroom and living accommodation. Behind it a stairway led down to the sally port *(p.23)*. A skirt of stone protected the natural sandstone at the foot of the tower from collapse or undermining.

As with the gatehouse, attackers had first to overcome the obstacles of drawbridge, gate and portcullis. Once inside they found themselves in a right-angled passage, with at least one more gate and portcullis still lying ahead of them. In the meantime, the defenders, in rooms or on walkways above, had the opportunity to rain down arrows and rocks - and, no doubt, boiling oil if they had it - through slits onto the attackers below. The shouldered arch of the window was similar to archways at Clifford's Tower, York (mid 13th century).

Great Hall

THE GREAT HALL, where the Lord of the Manor and his retinue dined, was on the first floor. Its windows overlooked the courtyard while its opposite wall, the curtain wall of the bailey, was solid. It had a stone flagged floor. It was approached by an outer staircase and an entrance hall known as the Presence Chamber. Most of what remains today is the wall of the ground floor cellar, which was used as a store-room. The cellar windowsill on the left has a groove for a wooden shutter. Two circular pillars in the cellar supported stone vaulting.

Seen from the bailey, a similar building called the Great Chamber adjoined the Hall on the left. The Presence Chamber stood to the right.

Great Hall (left) and
Presence Chamber, 1485.

The pillar base *(below left)* supported a small circular gallery. The round tower's finial *(below right, now in Wakefield Museum)*, is carved in a fleur-de-lys design, later adopted as the badge of Wakefield.

Presence Chamber

THE WINDOW of the Presence Chamber, which was sometimes referred to as a Lodging Chamber, overlooked the castle larder and kitchens.

A round tower *(see previous page)* stood at the courtyard corner of this building and it is possible that a square tower, part of the bailey's curtain wall defences, stood at the adjacent corner.

Larder

TWO HEARTHS were found in the small building next to the Presence Chamber, which has been identified as the larder. In 1322 a spot check of the castle's contents recorded that the larder contained carcases of beef, sides of bacon, measures of salt and casks of herring (an estimated 3,108 herrings in total!).

Alchemy

THE ROOM above the larder may have been used for alchemical experiments. A hearth, incorporating a stone shelf, in a corner of the bailey between the larder and the kitchen, may also have been used. Alchemists aimed to find an elixir of life and the Philosopher's Stone, which would transform base metals into gold. Digging in the barbican moat nearby, archaeologists found ceramic jars, beakers and cucurbits (gourd-shaped retorts), glass flasks and alembics (distillation apparatus). A few fragments were also found at the gatehouse.

Marks scratched on some of the alchemical vessels found in the Barbican ditch.
Detail from 'The Alchemist', after Adrian van Ostade, (1610-85) 19

Sandal's collection of alchemical vessels, at least 170 in total, was described by Stephen Moorhouse* as 'the largest and most complete assemblage known'. He suggests that 'the Sandal workshops were the result of an illegal enterprise by persons unknown.'

Kitchen

MASSIVE foundations, 32 feet (9.7m) square, mark the site of the 13th century kitchen. It had a pyramidal stone-tiled roof topped by a central timber louvre, which acted as a chimney. Two posts supported a spit over the hearth. Its drain emptied into the barbican moat. It replaced an earlier, smaller kitchen (16 feet x 13 feet, 5m x 4m) in timber and clay which stood in the bailey.

* *Sandal Castle Excavations 1964-1973*

Bakehouse

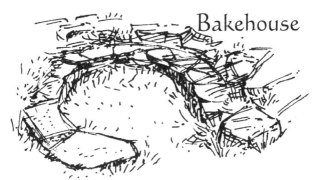

RICHARD III remodelled the bakehouse in the 1480s, adding a large oven to two much smaller circular ones.

The Sandal castle breakfast seems to have been popular. In his rules for the household, drawn up in June 1484, Richard III states;

'Item: My lord of Lincoln and my lord Morley be at oon brekefast, the children togeder at oon brekefast, such as be present of the counsaill at oon brekefast, and also that the household goo to dyner at the ferrest by 11 of the clok of the flessheday, &c'

But he adds; 'Item: that noo brekefastes be had in the house but suche as be assigned, &c.'

Drum Towers

THE TWIN drum towers, named for their shape, were built in the 13th century to provide yet another line of defence. They replaced the timber bridge across the moat which had originally connected the bailey and the keep.

Sally Port

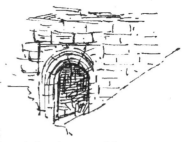

THE 1480s sally port (*right*) in the curtain wall, hidden in the moat near the drum towers, offered a secret back-door for the castle's defenders, enabling them to sally forth to make a surprise attack on the enemy. It was blocked on the outside during the Tudor period and was then used as a latrine, probably by the bakers who operated an oven set into the bailey bank nearby. Two damaged medieval stone mortars large vessels for grinding food - found in the sally port may have been used as chamber pots.

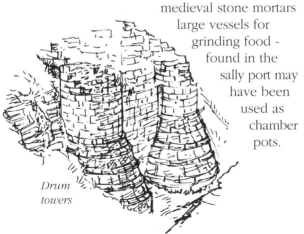

Drum towers

Stonework

The barbican was built on an outcrop of local sandstone, the **Oaks Rock.**

Diagonal **chisel marks** are typical of earlier stonework, for example on the gatehouse (*c.* 1250).

Later stonework on the barbican (1270) and on the drum towers has a smoother finish.

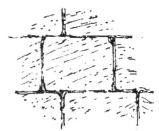

Oaks Rock dug from the moat was used as **infill** in the walls. Better quality stone for masonry may have been quarried at Woolley Edge.

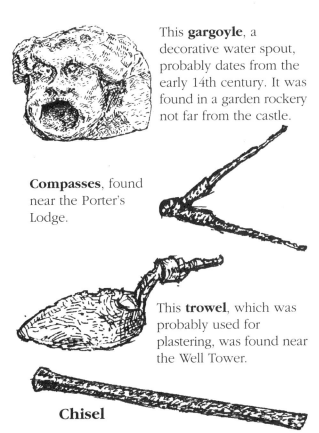

This **gargoyle**, a decorative water spout, probably dates from the early 14th century. It was found in a garden rockery not far from the castle.

Compasses, found near the Porter's Lodge.

This **trowel**, which was probably used for plastering, was found near the Well Tower.

Chisel

Post holes from the castle's timber buildings were found during the excavations, but no trace of them is visible today.

Building Boom

DURING THE 13th century, when the castle was rebuilt in stone, the old timber great hall was taken over by the construction workers. A lead-smelting hearth was installed inside. On the west side of the bailey, where the bakehouse would be built later, a roof tile kiln was constructed.

Stone masons set up their workshop in the old clay and timber castle kitchen. Workers were provided with bread and ale from an on-site oven and malt-kiln. The bread oven was near the main entrance to the bailey.

Spoil excavated from the barbican moat was used to raise the level of the bailey. As archaeologists dug through it they found the mud, now hardened, of the 13th century building site. A trackway had been preserved; the footprints of a horse and an ox yoked together that had been pulling a cart with a wheel-span of 4 feet were found.

John, 7th Earl de Warenne, *(c.1231-1304)* was the Lord of the Manor of Wakefield at the time. He was a warrior who played a part in campaigns against the Welsh and the Scots as well as in English baronial troubles. In 1270 Walter Giffard, Archbishop of York complained about the excessive demands that John was making on his Yorkshire tenants; a possible reference to the building boom at the castle. The illustration, taken from a seal, shows his grandson John, the 8th and last Earl de Warenne *(1286 - 1347)*.

Park

IN 1322 a 'certain forester and his boy*' were paid 3½ pence a day between them as keepers of the castle's park and woodland. In 1304 there were 30 acres of deer pasture in the park at Sandal. Not surprisingly, venison was frequently on the menu at the castle; archaeologists found that almost 40% of the animal bones from this period were from deer - mainly Fallow, but with some Red. By 1500 this had dropped to about 20%, and beef had replaced venison as the main meat. Pigs were grazed in woodland, so a plunge in pork consumption during the same period suggests a gradual clearance of trees.

*garcio; *which could mean either servant or boy*

Left; *Castle from Milnthorpe Lane, which was the medieval route of the Wakefield to London road.*

In 1566 surveyors calculated that there were sufficient trees in the park, or in Wakefield's outwood within two miles of the castle, to supply all the timber needed for repairs at that time. In 1270-1, when 60 oaks were needed for the construction of the barbican, timber was brought in by cart from the outwood and also, apparently, from Ossett, where the Lord of the Manor owned a large deer park, the New Park. In 1270-1 graves paid 5s 10d (29p) for 'keeping two sparrow-hawk nests in the wood, and carrying the same to the castle of Sandal.'

In 1304 fish kept in a small pond near the castle had died. A larger, 4½ acre, pond lay in the valley below. Herring, cod, oyster and mussels were eaten but no bones of freshwater fish were found in excavations of the medieval castle. Carp were eaten during the Civil War Siege.

In 1588 when Sir John Savile of Howley was appointed as constable, porter and steward of the castle, he was also given the post of 'park paler'. The paler's main task was to maintain the pale, a fence of wooden stakes, that kept the livestock inside the park.

Owners of Sandal Castle

1106   **William de Warenne**, 2nd earl, receives Manor of Wakefield from Henry I

1138   **William de Warenne**, 3rd earl *(died on a crusade)*

1148   **William de Blois**, 4th earl *(d. 1159)*

1164   **Hamelin de Plantagenet**, 5th earl

1202   **William de Warenne**, 6th earl

1240   **John de Warenne**, 7th earl

1304   **John de Warenne**, 8th earl *(d. 1347)*

1317   **Thomas, earl of Lancaster** *(takes the castle in a private war with John de Warenne)* executed at Pontefract after the Battle of Boroughbridge, 1322.

1326   **John** regains Sandal *(but loses it again, 1327-1334)*

1347   **Edmund de Langley**, 5th son of Edward III

1402   **Edward duke of York**

1415   **Richard duke of York** *(killed at the Battle of Wakefield, 1460)*

1460   **Edward duke of York** *(becomes Edward IV, 1461)*

1483   **Richard III** *(killed at the Battle of Bosworth, 1485)*

1485   The Crown as Duke of York

1566   Castle leased to **Edward Carey**, later to the Saviles

1638   Castle sold to **Francis Nevile** of Chevet

Civil War Seige

Basket-hilted sword

AT THE START of the English Civil War in 1642, a Royalist garrison occupied the castle, which by then was in a poor state of repair. They built stables, a workshop and a black-smith's forge in the corner of the bailey where the bakehouse had stood. Outer defences were constructed, including a crescent-shaped bastion to the south-east of the castle, outside the moat.

After a few months, the first Royalist commander, Major Ward, fell down a flight of stairs and broke his neck. His skeleton is probably one of the 9 Civil War burials found in excavations of the bailey. Early in 1645 Royalists came out of the castle to make a surprise attack on the besieging Roundheads, who were at prayer, killing 42 and taking 50 prisoner. In May of that year, a Royalist party which had gone out, so it's said, to collect may blossom was surprised by Roundheads and 8 were killed.

One of the cooking pots.

Clay pipes.

Archaeologists found fragments of two cooking pots next to the remains of a fire in the keep. Pieces of animal bone found with them suggest that soldiers were about to eat a stew when an attack brought part of the building crashing down. It has been calculated that the castle's 12 officers shared one cooking pot, one beer flask and one chamber pot between two of them, while their 88 men had to make do with one of each of these items between eight. Each man was issued with a pottery cup.

After the fall of Pontefract Castle in July 1645, the Roundheads brought in four large battery guns from Hull. After a heavy bombardment in September most of the castle lay in ruins. Terms of surrender were agreed *(right)*. On 30th April 1646 Parliament ordered the demolition of Sandal Castle.

Yellow-ware chamber pot, made by Robert Glover of Potovens, Wrenthorpe, for the Sandal garrison.

Articles of Rendition (extracts)

FIRST, it is agreed upon that the Governour of Sandall Castle himself in person with the rest of the Gentlemen Officers, and Souldiers shall have liberty to march to Welbeck* and to have a sufficient convoy, and foure dayes time to march thither.

All Officers, Gentlemen and Souldiers to the number of 12 to carry one sute of cloathes and the cloathes which they weare, the rest of the common men to have only the sute they weare, no more . . .

That two hostages of either party be given . . . that no man carry money out with them, which if it be found about any man, he is to remaine prisoner, but no man is to be searched after he come out of the Castle . . .

All Ammunition and provision of war, to be delivered, together with the Castle, which is to be surrendered by ten a clock tomorrow, being the first day of October . . .

Signed. Will Crooke, Tho. Harper,
(Majors in the Roundhead forces)
Jo. Benson *(Royalist Captain)* 30th September 1645

The Royalist stronghold at Welbeck House, Notts.

The Rise & Fall of Sandal Castle

c. **5000 b.c.**, Mesolithic hunters camp at Sandal.

? - *c.* **1106**, site is part of the open fields of the village of Sandal.

c. **1106 – 1138**, earthworks and timber castle constructed.

c. **1240 - 1270** castle rebuilt in stone.

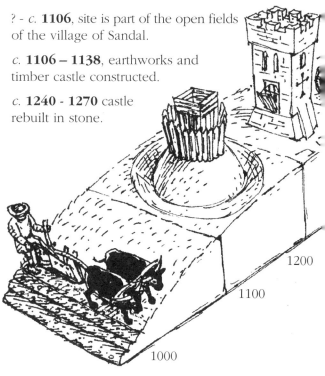

1200

1100

1000

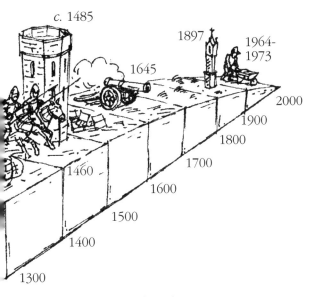

c. 1485

1897

1964-1973

1645

2000

1900

1800

1700

1600

1500

1460

1400

1300

1322, survey of castle's contents.

1460, 30th December, Battle of Wakefield.

1484, Richard III orders improvements to the castle.

1538 - 66, surveys reveal a castle in decline.

1645, civil war siege leaves castle in ruins.

1897, Victorian memorial to Richard Plantagenet at Manygates.

1964 - 1973, excavations at castle.

Acknowledgements

MY EXTENDED thanks to all who took part in the 1964 - 1973 excavations including Phil Mayes, Lawrence Butler and Stephen Moorhouse. Thanks also to Steve Chapman and to Pam Judkins, Wakefield MDC keeper of archaeology, who checked my manuscript.

Finds from the excavations can be seen at Wakefield Museum; my thanks to the staff there. The new visitor centre and the improved access to the earthworks were opened in September 2002 by archaeologist Julian Richards (who took part in the dig at Sandal in the 1970s).

Further Reading

Mayes, P. & Butler, L.A.S. 1983, *Sandal Castle* Excavations 1964-1973, Wakefield Historical Publications
Butler, Lawrence, 1991 *Sandal Castle, Wakefield, The History and Archaeology of a Medieval Castle*, Wakefield Historical Publications, ISBN 0-901869-31-7
Haigh, Phillip A., 1996, *The Battle of Wakefield* 1460, Sutton Publishing; ISBN: 0-750913-42-8
Dockray, Keith & Knowles, Richard, 1999, *The Battle of Wakefield*, Wakefield MDC.; Off-print from *The Ricardian*, the Journal of the Richard III Society, volume IX, number 117, June 1992.